learning. exploring. discovering. learn

Greece
Children's travel activity and keepsake book

Yassou!

tinytourists
explore discover learn

Yassou !

Hello! My name's Topher*
and I love adventures!

I'll be keeping you company on your journey through
this book. Look out for me, I'll be popping
up every now and again.

Each time you see me say
"Yah-soo" to say hello

Count how many times
you can spot me too...

*Topher is named after St. Chris**topher**, the patron saint for travellers who is known for keeping all those who travel safe from harm.

tinytourists is all about inspiring family travel and making the most of adventures; keeping travel meaningful and memorable, educational and fun. Visit us on Facebook to find out more and to join the tinytourists' community.

Written and Designed by Louise Amodio
Illustrated by Louise Amodio and Catherine Mantle
Cover Illustrations by Isabella (age 6), Bethany (age 9) and Emily (age 7).

Published by Beans and Joy Publishing Ltd as a product from Tiny Tourists Ltd, Great Britain.
www.beansandjoy.com

ISBN: 978-1-912293-00-1

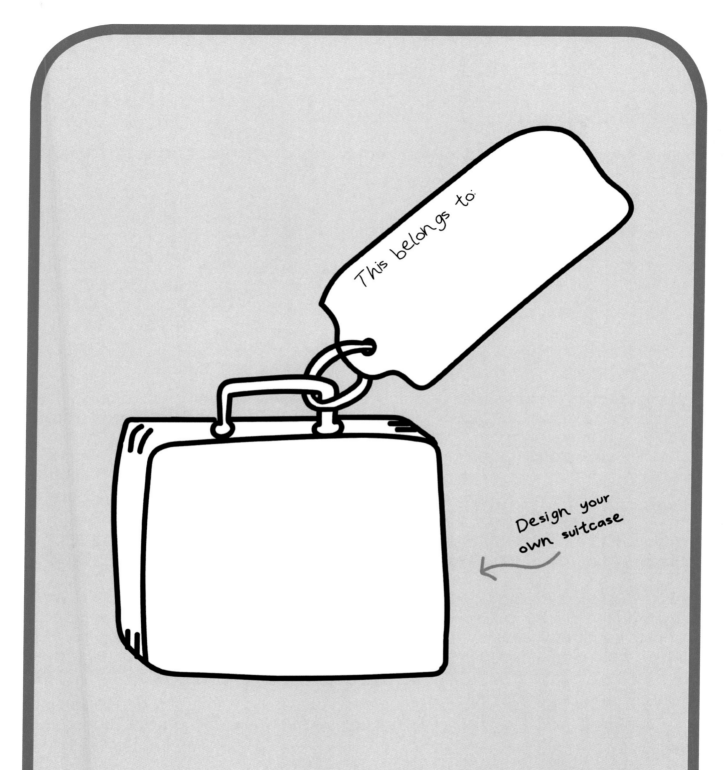

This belongs to:

Design your
own suitcase

Your adventure starts here

How to use this book

Welcome to your fun-packed travel activity book!

Look out for these symbols to tell you what type of activity you'll be doing so you can start to work independently:

 for writing and mark-making

 for drawing and colouring and being creative

Time to get started!

For the grown-ups to read:

Section 1: My Travel Log

Use this section to start thinking about your trip to Greece; when you're going, where you're going, who you're going with, what the weather be like, and what you'll pack in your suitcase. This will help form part of a lovely keepsake as well as practice your planning and organisational skills!

Section 2: Explorer Skills

This section is full of games and activities for a bit of Greece-themed fun. All are designed to support the National Curriculum and grouped into **Maths (p12-25)**, **Literacy (p26-36), and The World Around Us (p37-42)**. See index for more details.

Also included are some Greek words you might like to try out during your trip. We give you the english spelling, the phonetic spelling (what it sounds like), and the english translation to make things straightforward. Greek has its own alphabet which we haven't tried to master in this book, we've stuck to the roman alphabet.

phrase: yassou
say: (yah-soo)
meaning: hello

phrase: efcharisto
say: (ef-cha-ri-sto)
meaning: thank you

phrase: parakalo
say: (pah-rah-kah-loh)
meaning: please

Section 3: Memory Bank

This is where you can record all the memories from your trip. The perfect finishing touch to a lovely book of holiday memories; what you did, what you ate, what you saw, what you collected, and fun lists for recording the best bits and the worst bits.

Happy Travels!

My Travel Log

Me:

stick or draw your
picture here →

Where am I going?

Arrival:

Date: _____

Passport Stamp:

Departure:

Date: _____

Where am I going?

This is a map of Greece and her islands.
The capital city of Greece is Athens - can you spot it?

Find out where you are going on holiday and add it to the map:

Thessaloniki

Thassos

Mount
Olympus

Larissa

Volos

Corfu

Lesvos

Patrai

Athens

Kefalonia

Piraeus

Zante

Mykonos

Kos

Sparta

Santorini

Rhodes

Crete

How will I get there?

Find the transport you're using to get to Greece and colour it in:

What am I taking with me?

Draw the important things you've got packed in your suitcase:

valítsa
(vai-lista)
suitcase

Who am I going with?

Draw a picture of who you're going on holiday with in the frame below:

Example

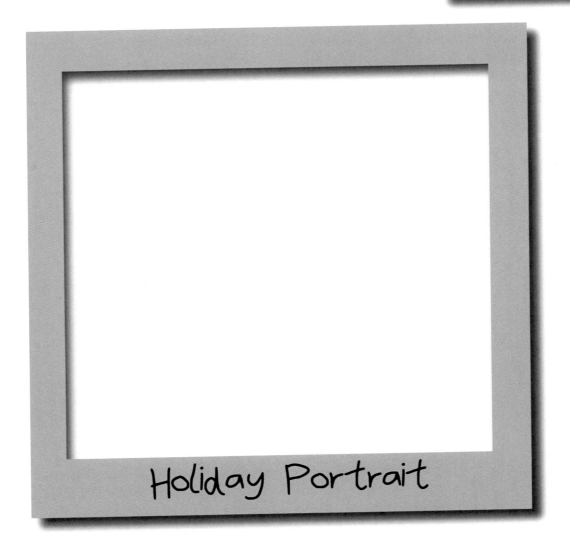

Holiday Portrait

I moúmia mou
(ee moomya moo)
My mummy

O bampas mou
(a bampas moo)
My daddy

What will the weather be like?

Draw a circle around the weather you think you'll have:

vréchei
(vreshee)
It's raining

échei liakáda
(day-she lakatha)
It's sunny

chionízei
(chion-eezee)
It's snowing

Explorer Skills

Problem-solving
(Maths)

Communicating
(Literacy)

Investigating
(The World Around Us)

"I Galanolefki"
(The Blue and White)

This is the Greek flag, with stripes of blue and white and a white cross.

Complete the flag below by **adding blue to the right places:**

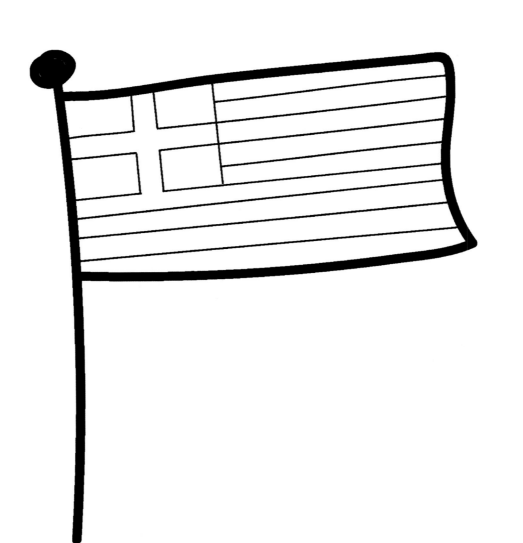

Blue Boats

Greece has 6,000 islands so you may see boats travelling in the seas around them.

Circle all the boats with blue sails below.
How many are there?

White sailboats

Circle all the boats with white sails below:

How many are there?

Design your own boat

What are your favourite colours? _____

Design the boat below in your own choice of colours:

Greek Salad 1-5

Greece enjoys the perfect weather to grow juicy red tomatoes, and olives and cucumbers. And is also home to lots of goats whose milk is used to make yummy feta cheese.

Count the greek salad ingredients below and circle the right number on the number line:

1 2 3 4 5

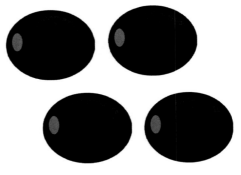

1 2 3 4 5

ellinikí saláta
(eliniki salata)
greek salad

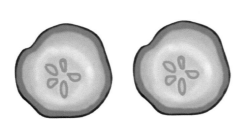

1 2 3 4 5

1 2 3 4 5

énas	dýo	tría	téssera	pénte
venas	vee-o	tree-a	vess-era	pen-deh
1	2	3	4	5

Greek Salad 1-10

Count the food and circle the right number below.
Which one do you think is your favourite?_____
Do you think this food is healthy or not healthy? _____

1 2 3 4 5 6 7 8 9 10

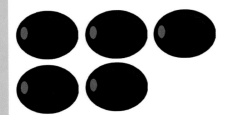

1 2 3 4 5 6 7 8 9 10

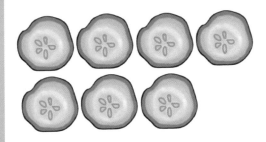

1 2 3 4 5 6 7 8 9 10

1 2 3 4 5 6 7 8 9 10

Counting Kebabs 1-5

Kebabs (Souvlaki) are one of the most popular street foods in Greece. They are tasty pieces of meat, cheese or vegetables put onto long sticks and then cooked.

Count the different kebabs below and circle the right number:

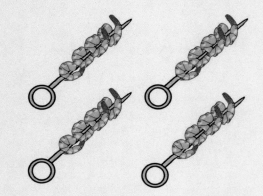

1 2 3 4 5

Garífalo souvláki
(vary-faloo soovliaki)
prawn kebab

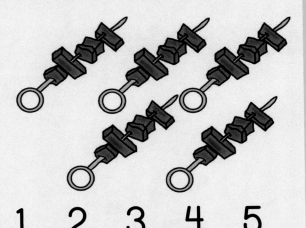

1 2 3 4 5

Arní souvláki
(panee soovliaki)
lamb kebab

1 2 3 4 5

Chaloúmi souvláki
(halloomi souvliaki)
halloumi kebab

1 2 3 4 5

Kotópoulo souvláki
(koto-poola souvliaki)
chicken kebab

Counting Kebabs 1-10

Count these kebabs and circle the right number below.

Have you tried any of these? Which is your favourite? _____

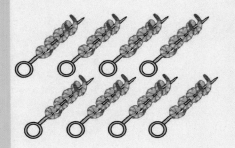

1 2 3 4 5 6 7 8 9 10

1 2 3 4 5 6 7 8 9 10

1 2 3 4 5 6 7 8 9 10

1 2 3 4 5 6 7 8 9 10

Greek Salad!

Traditional greek salad has many yummy ingredients;
tomatoes, cucumber, olives, feta cheese, onions.
You might get to try it on your travels to Greece.

Can you find the matching pairs amongst these ingredients?
Draw a line from one ingredient to the identical other:

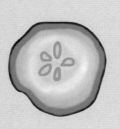

Greek favourites

Which have been your favourite foods so far?
Can you draw them on this plate?

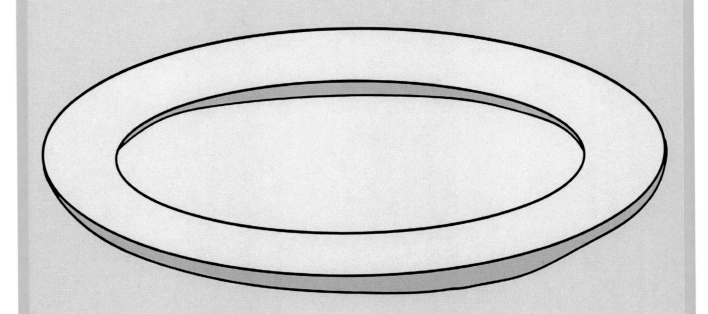

Greek Islands

Greece has a lot of islands! Its biggest is called Crete.

Can you spot the **smallest** island from the group below?

22

Smallest Island

Circle the **smallest** island on each of these rows:

Greek Church!

Greece can be very sunny and people often paint their houses white to reflect the heat away. On some islands you will find hundreds of white churches with blue roofs, or maybe other colours.

Have you seen any churches on your visit to Greece?
Can you **find the biggest** church on this page?

Biggest Church

Circle the **biggest** church on each of these rows:

Greek Churches

Greece's main religion is Christian Orthodox, and there are many churches and monasteries scattered all over Greece and her islands. In the Cyclades islands, churches nearly always have white walls and blue domed roofs.

Use your colouring pencils to **add some colour** to this picture. Do you want to colour in the roofs blue? Or choose a different colour?

The Parthenon

This is the Parthenon - a very very old temple that still stands on the sacred hill of Acropolis in the middle of Athens, the capital city of Greece. The Parthenon was built over 2,000 years ago and is dedicated to Athena, a Greek Goddess.

Use your colouring pencils to **add some colour** to this picture:

Olympic Rings

The Olympic Games started in Greece over 2,700 years ago and were performed to honour the Greek God, Zeus.

The olympic rings are the main symbol of the modern Olympic Games. They represent the continents that take part.

Can you **draw round each of these olympic rings?**
How many are there? _____

Can you **colour in** each of the rings below to match above?

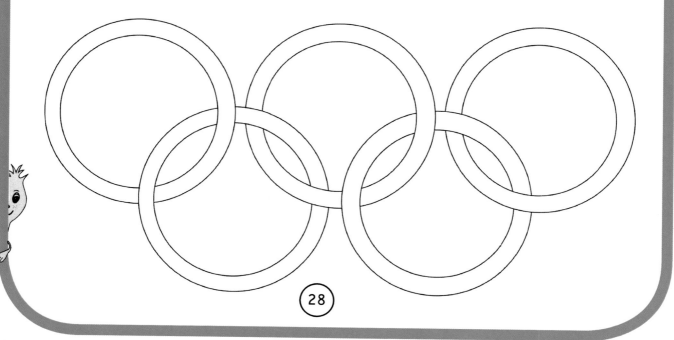

28

Olympic Rings

These Olympic Rings have lost their colour. Can you trace a line through this maze, touching each coloured ring with your pencil on your way?

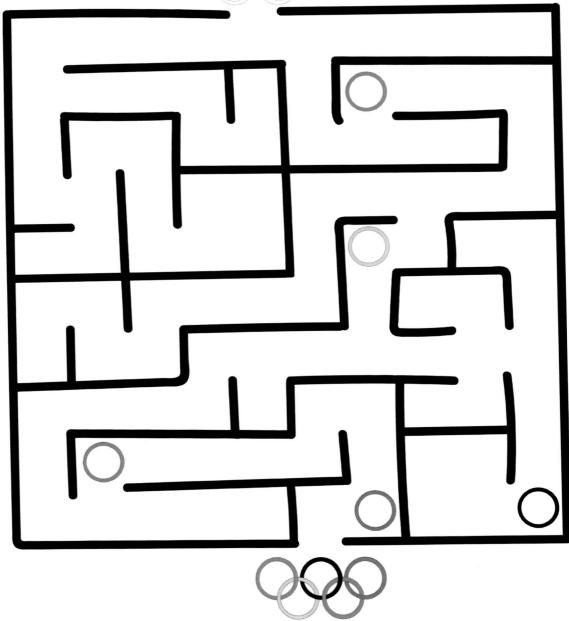

Running

One of the most popular sports to compete in in the Olympics is running. Who can run the fastest in your family? _____

Can you draw a line as quickly as you can through this maze from the runner to the finishing flag?

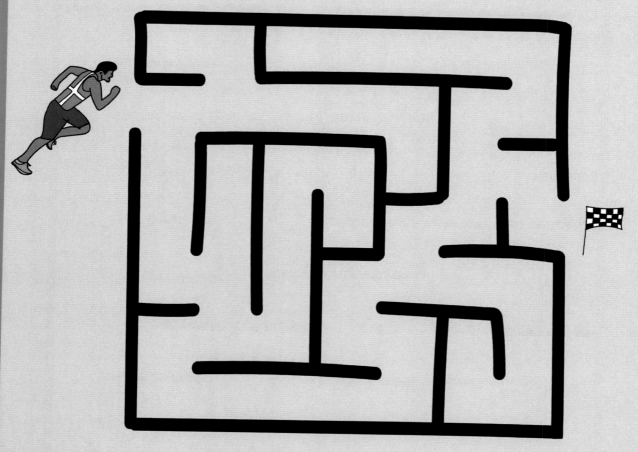

Throwing

Another set of olympic sports involves throwing various objects as far as you can!

Can you trace along the lines from these three shotputs to see how far they go?

How far can you throw a ball?

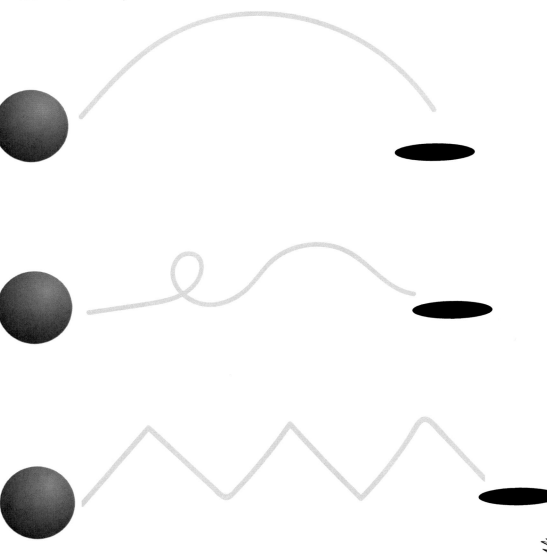

The God of the Skies

There are many Greek stories, called myths, about the Ancient Gods that some people believe rule the world.

The Greek God who is in charge of all the other Gods is called Zeus. Zeus has two brothers, Poseidon who rules the sea, and Hades who rules the Earth. Zeus rules the skies and lives at Mount Olympus, the highest mountain in Greece...and if he ever gets angry with any of the other Gods he throws a thunder bolt at them! He has a pretty bad temper.

Do you think when you hear some thunder it is Zeus throwing a thunderbolt at one of his naughty brothers?

Add a splash of colour

Colour this picture matching the colours opposite,
or in your own choice of colours.

If you were a Greek God would you want to be the ruler of the sky,
the earth or the sea?

Shape-search

Find the objects in this grid that look like circles and ovals.
How many are there of each?
Do you recognise any other shapes?

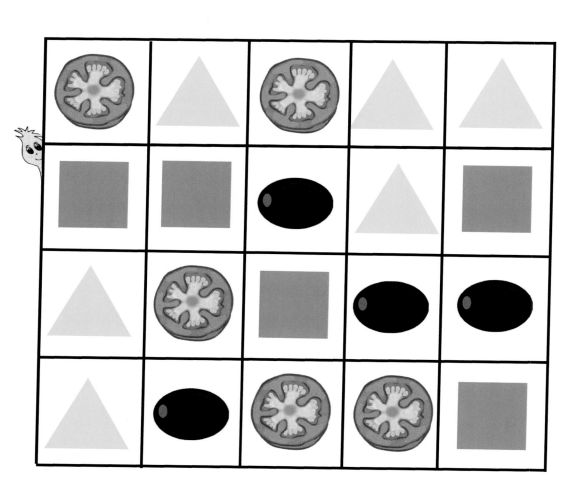

Letter-search - Greece

Find as many of these 3 letters in the grid as you can:

g_ r_ c_

g	c	r	g	c
r	g	r	c	c
r	s	g	c	r
c	g	g	c	r

Greek Vase

Many years ago, the Greek city of Athens was a major pottery-producing area and produced pots of all shapes and sizes.

Pottery makers would often draw pictures of stories on their pots. What's your favourite story? Can you decorate this pot with some pictures from your favourite story?

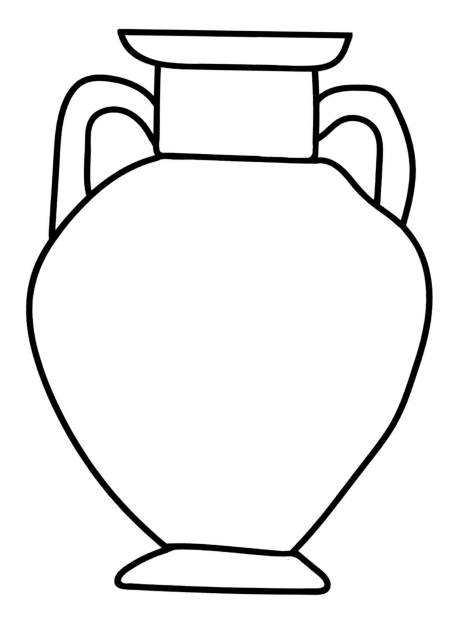

Spot the difference

Look along each row below and see if you can **find the vase that is different** to the others:

Musical Spot the Difference

This is a Greek Lyre - an instrument from the times of Ancient Greece.
It is said that the Greek Gods once made these out of tortoise shells!
Can you spot the 5 differences between these two Lyre?

Do you know any other instruments that have strings?

A Place to Stay

Where are you staying on your holiday in Greece? Is it a hotel? A house? A tent? A boat? A campervan? An apartment?

Can you **draw a picture** of it here?

Home Sweet Home

Can you **draw a picture** of where you live back at home?

What is different about this and your holiday home?

What do you know about Greece?

Can you circle some of the things you might see in Greece?
Which things do you think you might NOT see?

Memory Bank

Use this section to record and remember all the
things you've done, seen and tasted on your trip!

Draw, Write, Staple, Stick!

You may need a grown up to
help with some of the writing...

What have you eaten?

Draw some food you have eaten on holiday on the plate below. What was your favourite?

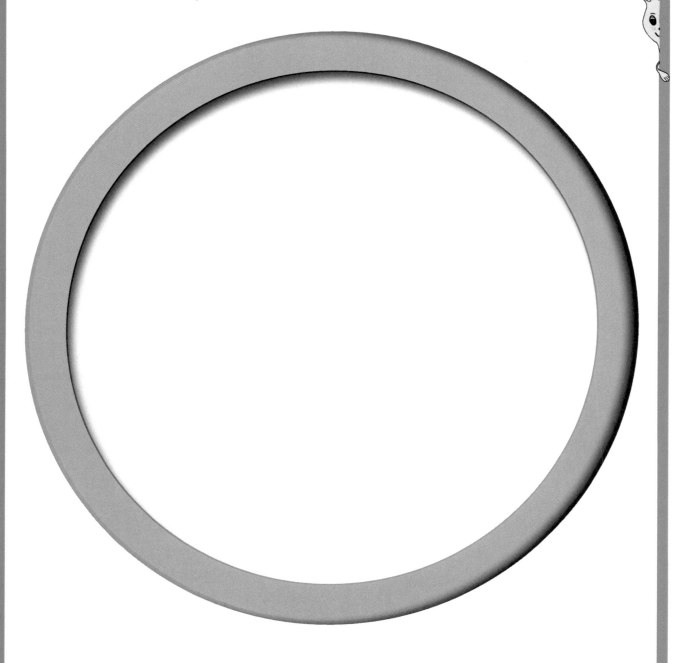

What adventures have you had?

Ask someone to help you **write a postcard** about your adventures, and design a nice stamp:

καρτ ποστάλ

Momento Collage

Stick bits and pieces on these pages that you've collected during your trip; favourite tickets, receipts, leaflets, drawings, flowers...

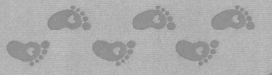

Daily Diary

Note down some of the different things you have done each day:

Monday

Tuesday

Wednesday

Thursday

Friday

Saturday

Sunday

Memory Gallery

Draw pictures or doodles of any special memories:

Worst 5

What have been the **worst** five things about your trip?

_____

_____

_____

_____

_____

Top 5

What have been the **best** five things about your trip?

Index

(what's in this book and where you can find it)

Antio sas

(goodbye)

I hope you enjoyed your adventure and completing this book along the way.

How many times did you spot me?

_____

Keep safe!
Love from
Topher xx

Where would you like to go next?

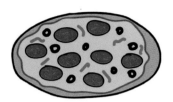

Italy

USA

Spain

France

Egypt

China

UK

Australia

South Africa

Thailand

Mexico

Finland